DREAM MACHINE

Can you see
what I see?
Five cards, a bike,
three soccer balls,
a spotted owl,
striped overalls,
an elephant,
a dog asleep,
a dinosaur tail,
seven white sheep,
a yo-yo, a boat,
a can, a jar,
a lightning bolt
on a little red car!

Can you see
what I see?
Two dominoes,
a lion king,
a puzzle piece,
a yo-yo string,
three crayons, a duck,
a flowerpot,
a bus, a bow,
an astronaut,
a hot dog bun,
a radio,
a speedy roadster
on the go!

Can you see
what I see?
A key,
three sneakers,
seven dice,
a rocking chair,
a pig, three mice,
a windblown scarf,
a charming toad,
a roadster on
a cardboard road,
a musical monkey
strumming a tune,
a rolling marble,
a magical moon!

Can you see
what I see?
Five puzzle pieces,
a ruler, a queen,
a hand that points
to number thirteen,
six pencils, a cow,
a bunny, four birds,
a catchy slogan
with two rhyming words,
a girl with a bow,
a hand in a pocket,
a spoon on a plate,
a man in a rocket!

Can you see
what I see?
A man in a helmet,
a man in a hat,
a watering can,
a curious cat,
a candle,
three matches,
a blue bird, a bell,
a pencil, a wrench,
two thimbles, a shell,
the eye of a needle,
a mouse that is red,
a car in for service,
DREAM CITY ahead!

Can you see
what I see?
A bicycle frame,
two alarm clocks,
a watchband buckle,
three padlocks,
a pair of scissors,
a star, two phones,
four keys, a whistle,
five traffic cones,
a DANGER sign,
a car on springs,
an upside-down boy,
and two yellow wings!

Can you see
what I see?
A big red star,
two crescent moons,
a ketchup bottle,
a clock, three spoons,
a big blue eye,
the number nine,
a playing card,
a parking sign,
a domino,
a yellow die,
an arrow pointing
toward the sky!

Can you see
what I see?
A silver phone,
a yellow funnel,
a red jet-car
inside a tunnel,
a shuttlecock,
a filling station,
a billboard
for a space vacation,
the planet Earth,
a fish, red thread,
a salt-shaker laser
on a robot head!

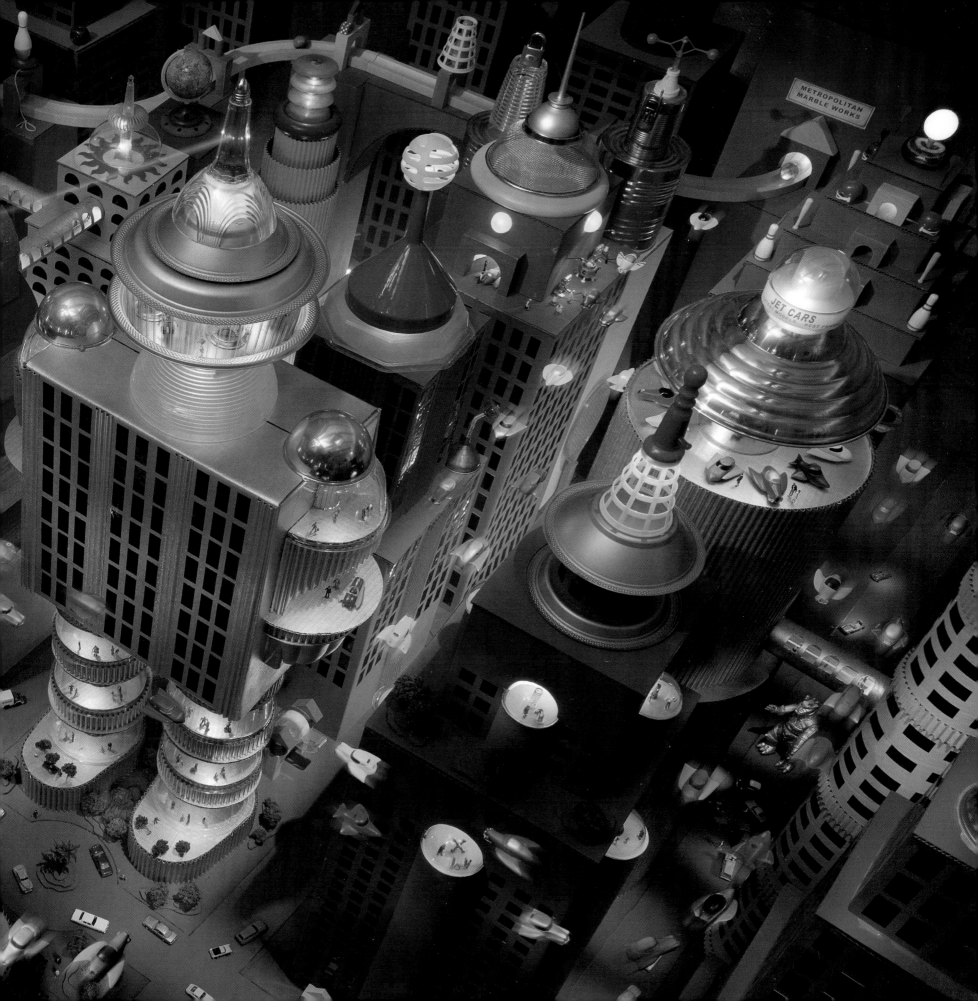

Can you see
what I see?
A fire hydrant,
a bottle-cap hat,
a domino six,
a baseball bat,
a comb, a tortoise,
a teapot spout,
a mouse on wheels
roaming about,
binoculars,
a looping string,
a dream machine
in a ruby ring!

Can you see
what I see?
A two-pronged plug,
a star, a fan,
fifteen cents,
a red-tipped can,
a lightning bolt,
antenna ears,
an hourglass that's
turned by gears,
a dartboard dial,
a phone connected —
now follow the maze
to the screen selected!

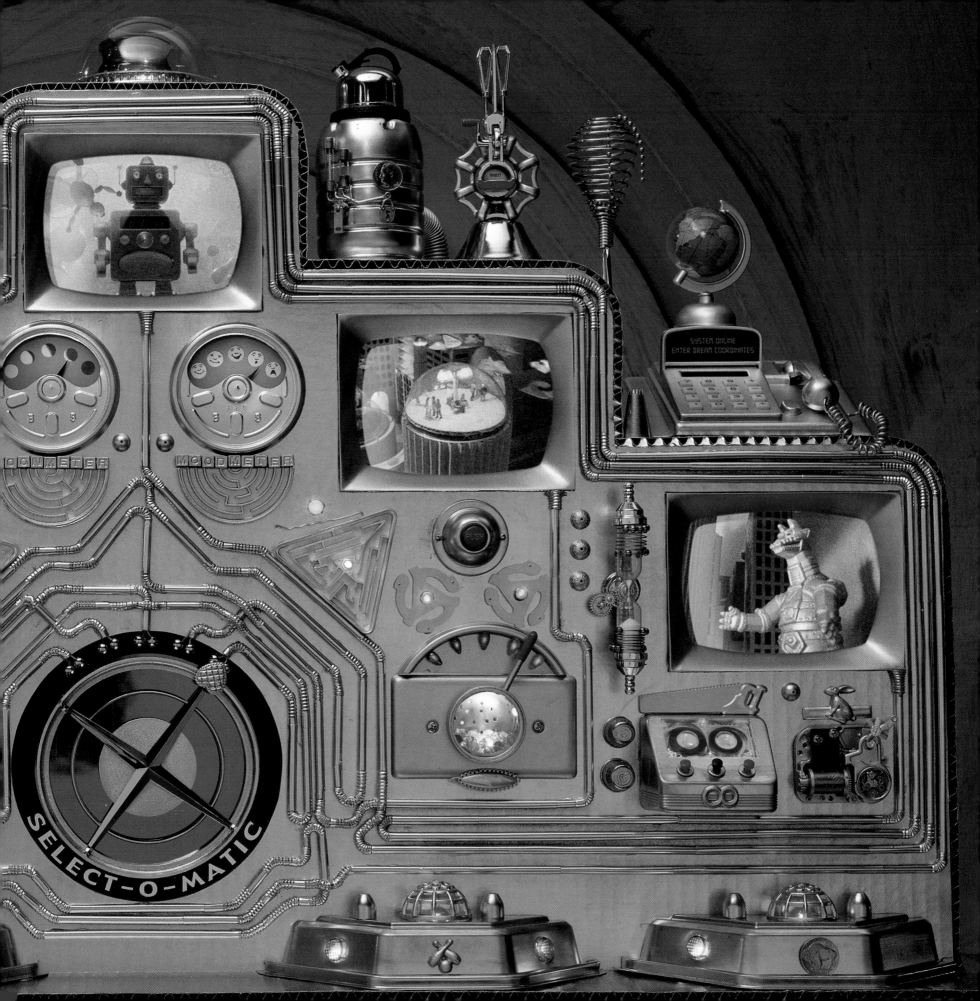

Can you see
what I see?
A football helmet,
a lamp, a skate,
a dog, a horse,
the number eight,
a battleship,
a jack, a die,
a domino,
the letter Y,
a spinning Earth,
a silver dime,
six forty-five —
it's wake-up time!

Can you see
what I see?
Five bowling pins,
a paper clip,
two airplanes,
a rocket ship,
a bone, a bat,
a sleepy dog,
a butterfly,
three cats, a frog,
a golden sun,
two skies of blue,
a bird that sings
cock-a-doodle-do!